Why Hidden?

Divine Hiddenness

Love

&

Revelation

by

Richard H. Corrigan

First Published in 2007 by The Parmenion Press, New York.
2 Penn Plaza
Manhattan
Garment District/ Madison Square Garden
New York
10121-1590

Library of Congress Cataloguing-in-Publication Data
    Corrigan, Richard H.
    Why Hidden? Divine Hiddenness, Love & Revelation
    First Published: 2007
    Includes Bibliographical References
    ISBN 978-0-6151-7183-8
    1. Why Hidden   I. Title

Editor: Louis Gardner

Proofreader: Adrienne Crippen

Cover Design: Pullman Designs

Typeset in Cambria

Printed in the United States of America

For my mother, Irene Jennings,

Who Always Encouraged Me

&

Mary Farrell

Who Always Believed in Me

Acknowledgements

I would like to thank my philosophical mentors: Rowland Stout, Brendan Purcell and the late Gerry Hanratty. Thanks too to my family and the Farrells for their support, love and friendship. I would also like to express my gratitude to the philosophers and theologians whose work has served as such an inspiration. Finally, I would like to thank everyone at the Parmenion Press, without whom this work would not have been possible.

Contents:

1
Introduction

The purpose of this book is to outline the principal difficulties that the 'hiddenness' of God poses, and to offer solutions to the question of why God does not incontrovertibly and indubitably reveal His existence to everyone.

It is prudent to begin by delineating the meaning of the proposition 'God is hidden'. The God with which I will be concerned is the Judeo-Christian deity of the Old and New Testaments. I will, therefore, offer a broad definition of the pertinent characteristics of the God that is traditionally understood to be the originator of the world in the Biblical account of creation. God is pure spirit, omnipotent, omniscient, eternal, uncreated, necessary and the ultimate personification of love and perfection. Furthermore, He desires a relationship with those creatures that He has created in His own likeness, and offers them gifts and assistance, as a measure of His unmerited love.

However, we shall see that even though this description offers a basic depiction of God, it is far from exhaustive and, even among Christians, the actual ways in which these attributes become manifest have been the subject of prolonged argument. The above account is merely intended to serve as a basic model, which is generally held to be uncontroversial in its broad strokes (except perhaps for the idea of unmerited love, which I will return to). When I speak in the forthcoming discussion of various arguments for and against the existence of God, it is an entity that fits this description that is being alluded to, unless otherwise stipulated.

Aiken has remarked:

> Logically, there is no reason why an almighty and omniscient being might not be a perfect stinker.[1]

This helps to illustrate the fact that belief in the existence of the Judeo-Christian God is a specific interpretation of divinity that is open to objection. Whilst one might subscribe to the belief that there is a God and that He is the origin of creation, there is no *necessary* reason to suppose that He is a supremely good being. One could argue, in traditional fashion, that God, as the ultimate perfection, must be that of which nothing greater can be conceived and, because good is greater than evil, God must be the ultimate good. However, the characteristics of

---

[1] Aiken, *God and Evil: a study of some relations between faith and morals*, 1958, p. 82.

omniscience and omnipotence do not logically entail that their subject be good. For this reason, the Christian must explain why the God of creation is also the God of love and justice.

There are various strategies that attempt to accomplish this end. For example, it can be claimed that even the individual who does not have the intellectual apparatus to formulate complicated philosophical argument may see evidence of the goodness of God in his everyday environment, and for this reason you should not doubt that God is good. Or, if you open yourself to the love of God, you can feel it in the world around you and you can become infused with it. For the Christian who has had such experiences, there is no need of further justification of his belief, but if he needed it, the authority the Church and the teachings of the Gospels would offer further reinforcement.

In the past, there have been various attempts to show that the existence of God can be proven through natural theology. I will attempt to show that there is a misunderstanding in the way that critics have traditionally read these proofs and dismissed them. This is because the matter rests on the adoption of a particular epistemic point of view. Suffice it to say for now, that we must consider Hume's point when he asserted that, if we attempt to read the existence of God from nature, there is no compelling reason to assume that He has positive characteristics rather than negative ones, that He is infinite rather than finite, that He is perfect rather than fallible, that He is ultimate as opposed to common, or that indeed He must conform to any of the attributes that I listed in the description proposed above.[2] We should of course bear in mind that when we attempt to 'read' anything from nature in the Humean sense, there will invariably be presuppositions in the process (for one will have to employ a conception of nature that has already been accepted before initiating the endeavour, and what the theist sees in nature is not necessarily the same as what the atheistic naturalist sees).[3] This point conveniently leads us to the question of divine hiddenness.[4]

---

[2] *Dialogues*, V. See also Hick, *The Existence of God*, 1964.

[3] I am differentiating between the naturalist and the atheist. Whilst both do not believe in God the former has given the matter serious consideration on its own terms whereas this is not necessarily true of the latter. Thus the naturalist may be the scientist who believes that all things can be explained by science without ever having seriously entertained the possibility of a spiritual element to reality.1

[4] This term is given qualification below.

Given that it is possible that we can be mistaken about the attributes of God, or can deny that He exists altogether, we must surely ask 'why it is that He remains hidden?' Why does God not make His existence obvious through some miraculous event or revelation that can be objectively verified? Why does He leave us in doubt as to whether we have misinterpreted His nature or even imagined Him as the result of superstition? Why does God hide from us? How does He hide from us? If, as the Christian insists, we must freely co-operate in the process of our own redemption, and if this freedom is dependent on belief in God, then surely there must be some way for us to come to that belief irrespective of our current opinion on theism (more on this topic will follow).

It seems that part of the ambiguity about a hidden God is that it is impossible to offer empirical verification of any propositions pertaining to Him. This can lead to scepticism regarding the nature of divinity and the renunciation of theistic interpretations of reality. From a theistic point of view, we are also left in the lamentable situation that, if God exists, we have certain responsibilities and duties towards Him, no one is exempt from these obligations, and yet many do not believe in Him. Yet how are we to effect the conversion of those that refuse to believe, or cannot make themselves believe, in a hidden God of love? Furthermore, if the Christian God exists, then those that do not surrender themselves to His decrees will be subject to judgment and punishment. How can we reconcile this state of affairs with a God that loves us, and wishes us to enter into a personal relationship with Him? Why would a God that wants to save us remain so veiled in mystery?

What exactly does it mean to say that God is 'hidden'? Luther offers us some illumination on this point. He believes that there are five distinct ways or areas in which God remains hidden. God hides in the darkness of faith, in light inaccessible, in the mystery of the incarnation, in the Church and the Blessed Virgin, and in the Eucharist.[5] In the forthcoming discussion I will focus primarily on the first of these, 'the darkness of faith' – the faith that guarantees no certainty, the faith that may make us passionately interested in God, the faith that may lead to substantive religious conversion, and the lack of faith that leads to atheism. It is important to remember that the term 'hidden' does not automatically exclude knowledge of that which is hidden. One may know of the

---

[5] McKim, *The Hiddenness of God*, 1990, p. 265.

existence of something, be totally convinced of its reality, and yet accept that it will indefinitely remain beyond our abilities to understand or perceive in its *totality*. Thus, to say that God is hidden is not to say that it is impossible to know with certainty many things about Him.

In *What the Hiddenness of God Reveals* Schellenberg's Sceptic states the following:

> 'God is hidden' can be seen as equivalent to the (inclusive) disjunction of the following claims: '(A) Some *theistic experience* - a state of affairs consisting in someone apparently becoming aware of the presence of God in some way - that could obtain or is desirable if God exists is *unavailable* to someone (perhaps each of us). (B) Some *theistic proposition* - some proposition equivalent to, entailing, or problifying theism, or bearing one of these relations to a full or partial explication or theological development of theism — is *epistemically nonsecured* or *epistemically indeterminate* for someone (perhaps each of us): that is to say, either not known (or not reasonably believed) to be true, or not known (or not reasonably believed) either to be true or to be false.'[6]

This gives us a rudimentary understanding of what is entailed in the proposition – but we shall see that the implications of the nature of divine disclosure (or the lack thereof) give rise to many related existential, religious and epistemological questions. I will now proceed to examine how divine hiddenness affects us, exactly what it entails, and the various strategies available to us to make God less hidden.

---

[6] Schellenberg, *What the Hiddenness of God Reveals*, 2002, p. 142.

2
A Lack of Evidence?

What exactly do critics of theism intend when they censure the fact that God does not provide convincing evidence of His existence? Exactly what would enable sceptics or atheists to come to belief in God? Some have insisted that what is needed is a form of manifestation that would leave it impossible to doubt the veracity of the being of God. What form then should this manifestation exhibit? Dilley offers us the criteria that he would deem satisfactory for such a universal revelation:

> What I have in mind as convincing demonstrations are public visible manifestations in which the supernatural powers of God are abundantly illustrated by appropriate wonder-working.[7]

This is a demand that has been echoed by many contemporary critics. Surely for many, whether of a religious persuasion or an avowed atheist, this is a question that has arisen, and which has significance in our lives. If God were to offer such a demonstration, would we be sufficiently impressed to follow His proscriptions in Scripture (or would we be led to Christianity at all)? Would it be enough for us to become devout theists? How would all of this affect the free exercise of our wills? Would they be enhanced by this display and be more prone to correct action, whilst still retaining those essentials that make them autonomous, responsible and free? Alternatively, would their independence be obliterated by the grandeur of the miracle?

Aquinas too believed in the importance of demonstrating the existence of God:

> …if we do not demonstrate that God exists, all consideration of divine things is necessarily suppressed.[8]

He devoted much energy to establishing, through natural theology, some foundation from which it would be possible to progress to knowledge of the divine. Aquinas did not claim that demonstrating the existence of God would allow us to perceive the many aspects of the divine personality which are

---

[7] Dilley, *Fool-Proof Proofs of God?*, 1977.
[8] Aquinas, *Summa Contra Gentiles*, Book One: God, Chap. 9: 5.

manifold, and at times mysteriously in opposition (for example, the God of love being also the God of wrath and so forth). This is a point that he clarifies when he states,

> God's effects, therefore, can serve to demonstrate that God exists, even though they cannot help us to know Him comprehensively."[9]

However, the 'proofs' of natural theology are not sufficiently forceful to meet the demands of philosophers such as Dilley.

What it appears we would need to provide is some empirical method of validating the existence of the divine. This method would have to be universally available and yield the same incontrovertible result – namely that the evidence would necessarily be assented to as providing irrefutable proof of the existence of God. If we were to come to knowledge of the divine through some inner state of awareness, that inner state would have to be sufficiently epistemically forceful to exclude the possibility of doubting its veracity and content. Psychological awareness of God, as sufficient proof for Dilley, would have to be a common and indubitable experience of the divine. The privileged experiences of mystics would not offer satisfactory proof, as their reliability could only be vouched for by those few who experience them, and could not be subjected to an empirical method of validation. It appears that what we are left with is the demand that we adopt an all-or-nothing approach.

As John Hick notes:

> It is doubtless true as a matter of psychological fact that a sufficiently impressive series of such happenings, if personally witnessed, would move almost anyone, however sceptical, to believe in God. But no general proof of divine existence, valid for those who have not experienced such events, can be based upon this fact.[10]

Keller adds the qualification that if some phenomenon occurred such that it could not be explained in any other reasonable way as anything other then an act of God, and

---

[9] Aquinas, *Summa Theologiae*, la, 2, 2.3
[10] Hick, *Philosophy of Religion*, 1973, p. 29.

...if everyone always saw or heard the same message about a particular situation, I think *most*[11] people would ascribe it to God.[12]

With Keller's statement we begin to see the main question that arises in relation to any possible formulation of a 'definitive proof' of God's existence - what exact form would this phenomenon take, if it were to be beyond doubt for *everyone*?

The Bible recounts the story of Lazarus – even when he had risen from the dead many of those who later witnessed his resurrection failed to believe in God as a consequence; even though there was no other conceivable way for them to explain what had occurred (I am not here intending to say that this was incontrovertible proof, I am merely suggesting that, if someone does not want to believe, they can always find a way to justify this stance).

Garcia points out the fact that much of the literature on hiddenness suffers from a thin conception of faith. Many such writers reach the conclusion that,

...if the faith that leads to our true end of union with God is largely a cognitive matter, then enabling persons to come to faith should be a relatively straightforward and easy task.[13]

Drange is a proponent of a similar view and states that people naturally want to know the truth, and knowing the truth is a good thing, so God should simply reveal it to them.[14] This demand is easy to make but agreeing on conditions that would satisfy it proves more complicated.

However, the problem is that to insist on an empirically verifiable demonstration is to allow the presupposition that the object to be experienced is of a type that could fall within the scope of the natural sciences. There are many things that we take as being certain that are not available for such scrutiny. For example, we take it as a given that certain people love us, yet love

---

[11] Italics are mine.
[12] Keller, *The Hiddenness of God and the Problem of Evil*, 1995. p. 21.
[13] Garcia, *St. John of the Cross and the Necessity of Divine Hiddenness*, 2002. p. 88.
[14] Drange, *Nonbelief and Evil*, 1998.

is not an experience that can be objectively verified in the fashion suggested above – in virtue of this, are we take it for granted that it can have no reality? The simple answer must be surely 'no'.

John Baille draws our attention to the fact in Biblical terms the man of faith does not need public demonstrations of the existence of God, as such 'proofs' are superfluous. In the Bible, at no point are we offered some overwhelming proof of the divine, even though this book is the foundation of many strands of Western religion and is accepted by them as the word of God (through his prophets). In it, as in the core books of many religious systems, the existence of God is taken as a given.

The ancient writers of the Bible believed that they had direct contact with the divine in their everyday environment and experience. God was as much a part of the reality that they experienced as the physical things that were available to their senses. For many of the prophets, and their followers, the various moods of nature were stamped with the mark of God; the success of their armies was a sign of God's pleasure and their defeat a sign of His wrath. The existence of God was not thought of as the product of an inferential move in interpretation, but as a given that was witnessed without doubt. The psalmist might often lament that God does not show Himself, but he never doubts that God does in fact exist.

For many true religious believers the problem of an unambiguous divine disclosure is an illusion, why does God need to show Himself in some empirically observable fashion, when (in their opinion) He has already given ample evidence of His existence? Furthermore, to some it would seem impertinent to even suggest that God should simply produce miracles and wonders on demand, as though He should be dictated to by the insistence of man. As one of Schellenberg's characters notes:

> Surely we get into the old problem of the pot telling the potter what to do if we expect God to produce such knowledge: God is under no obligation to do any such thing.[15]

As Schellenberg is all too aware, this is not an uncontroversial claim. Even though an omnipotent God obviously cannot be forced to do

---

[15] Schellenberg, *What the Hiddenness of God Reveals*, 2002. p. 36.

anything that he does not desire, there still remains the question as to whether there is an obligation for Him to reveal Himself, even if he does not have to do so. This is a point that warrants further discussion in due course.

I will now return to the issue of what exact form an unambiguous proof of divinity should take. Given the empiricists' methodological restrictions it is hard to imagine an empirical proof of God that would be both universally available and accepted without exception.[16]

If God were to perform some great miracle that was unprecedented in its grandeur, what exactly would this achieve? Would everyone automatically concur with the view that the miracle was the product of God's direct intervention in human affairs? Would there be other possibilities of interpretation? It is very difficult, if not impossible, to imagine the form that a miracle would have to exhibit if it were to force cognitive assent to the fact that it was a miracle. Miracles by their very nature are open to various interpretations. A religious origin is never necessarily the only way to interpret a given state of affairs, even if the state of affairs would generally be affirmed to be extremely anomalous.[17] Naturalistic[18] interpretations can be lent to any empirically observable state of affairs, even if the possibility of the natural occurrence of that state of affairs is almost non-existent. Any probability, no matter how small, is all that is required, and, furthermore, as one may simply insist that the scientific methodology necessary to give an empirically verifiable proof of the origin of an occurrence has not yet been developed (but it still *can* be developed). Via this route, it can be insisted that any occurrence has a naturalistic explanation, even if we do not yet have the theoretical or observational apparatus that would offer a satisfactory account of it. Peter Van Inwagen makes this point as follows:

> What you are saying seems to come down to this. You demand that God, in order to make His existence believable, cause some particular, unmistakable sign to occur somewhere in the world of

---

[16] Dilley, *Fool-proof Proofs of God?*, 1977. p. 6.

[17] See Murray, *Deus Absconditus*, 2002. p. 142

[18] By naturalistic I mean interpretations that conform to the methodologies of the natural sciences. Similarly, in the forthcoming discussion when I speak of something 'natural' in this context, I mean something empirically verifiable.

space and time. But when you hear a story of some event that would have been such a sign if it had actually occurred, you refuse, on epistemological grounds, to believe the story... First, these signs you want to place in the world would have to recur periodically, or, after a few generations had passed, people like you would say that the stories about the signs had grown in the telling – perhaps from the seed of an astronomical prodigy that, remarkable as it was had some purely natural explanation. We can imagine no sign that would have to be the work of a necessary, omnipresent, omnipotent being. Any sign you imagine you could also imagine to be the product of a contingent, locally present being whose powers, though vastly greater than ours, are finite.[19]

We must therefore conclude that any such proof would only offer evidence of the divine to those whose epistemology would allow such an interpretation.

Such reasoning is not a modern evolution. The authors of the Gospels were sensitive to this fact also. John writes:

After Jesus said this, he departed and hid from them. Although he had performed many signs in their presence, they did not believe in Him.[20]

Ferreira believes that to attempt to offer an empirically verifiable fool-proof proof of God's existence is to:

...assume a grammar which treats God as qualitatively similar to other things which could reveal themselves, or let themselves be revealed.[21]

God is not a physical entity that naturally has physically observable

---

[19] Van Inwagen, *What is the Problem of the Hiddenness of God?*, 2002. p. 28-29.
[20] John. 12:36-37.
[21] Ferreira, *A Kierkegaardian View of Divine Hiddenness*, 2002. p. 177.

characteristics, nor do His actions produce results that can be unambiguously accredited to Him by everyone. The empirical evidence that would be produced by the effects of a miracle would not necessarily offer sufficient proof to everyone of the existence of God. How then does the Christian know that His faith has not been misplaced? How will the atheist be sure that His beliefs have been mistaken if God exists? The Christian faith, along with the faith systems of many other religions, has definite beliefs about the salvation of mankind in the kingdom of God and of the continuation of the soul in some non-material incarnation.[22] At the end of days, it seems that the truth of the proposition that God exists will be made obvious to all; but this offers little consolation to the sceptic who is unwilling to postpone the question indefinitely.

It is important to take into consideration the nature of religious belief. If miracles were produced by God every time that someone's faith began to lapse, then the nature of faith would be radically transformed. Faith is an intensely personal experience that has a huge existential impact on the devotee. One of the essential aspects of faith is an element of freedom in our attitude to God. If there was absolute mathematical or psychological certainty of the existence of the divine then the character of our relationship with God would be significantly altered, and not necessarily for the better.

Christianity teaches that the relationship that God wants with us is one of reciprocal love, trust and moral integrity. A physical manifestation of God's existence is no guarantee that we would be brought any closer to accomplishing this goal. Furthermore, even if miracles were to effect an increase in the number of people who believe in God, there is no way that the external appearance of a particular sign or event would prove conclusively the nature of the being who brought about the occurrence.[23] Even the devil may enact a virtuous sign to serve an evil end. It should also be noted that, depending on the type of freedom that God values in man, it may be impossible for Him to give us an unambiguous proof of His existence, while still ensuring that we retain that freedom.

I have briefly alluded to God's purposes for mankind, and His desire for us to form a relationship with Him. This is a topic that I will proceed to cover to a much greater extent. For now, I would draw attention to Jesus'

---

[22] For a further discussion of this issue see Hick 1973. p. 93.
[23] See Keller, *The Hiddenness of God and the Problem of Evil*, 1995.

remark that "an evil and adulterous generation seeks a sign."[24] Jesus is suggesting that there is something offensive to God in the demand that the truth of His existence and nature be revealed in some spectacular fashion. The Christian understanding of our teleological purpose is that we should come to love God and do His bidding, because we find it the most rewarding thing to do and, more significantly, because it is what we choose to do.

For the Christian, God does not want us to merely become cognitively aware of His existence; He can never be experienced as a thing among the other things of the world. The way that we come to know Him must be internally (spiritually and morally) and existentially significant. God does not want us to just acknowledge His existence; He wants us to participate in the process of our redemption; so that we can fully appreciate the true nature of divinity.

Moser points out that there is a difference between morally significant and morally impotent miraculous signs.

> Morally impotent miraculous signs can entertain people but cannot transform their moral character. Morally transforming signs, in contrast, change one's moral character toward the moral character of God.[25]

I would suggest that, for the sceptic, the most that a miraculous sign could affect is spectacular awe or a conversion based on the wrong motivation. We will see that the reasoning behind our approaching the divine is especially important.

One might insist that we have not yet addressed the question of why God performs miracles in some instances and not in others, why He effects conversions in some via the media of external signs, while leaving others in doubt. Van Steenberg asserts that:

> ...the supernatural interventions of Providence (revelation, prophecies, miracles, apparitions, mystical phenomena and, *a*

---

[24] Matthew. 12:39.
[25] Moser, *Cognitive Idolatry and Divine Hiding,* 2002.

fortiori, the ordinary intervention of grace under all its forms), these always take place with the dignity and discretion that become the divine action.[26]

In response, I would briefly draw attention to Moser's reply:

God restrains divine manifestations, at least for a time, to at least some humans to enhance satisfaction of God's own diverse morally serious and loving purposes regarding humans… the variation is determined by God's purposes, or intentions.[27]

These are points that I will consider in much greater detail in the coming discussion. In closing this chapter I would draw attention to the fact that although there are many sceptics who believe that God should provide a universally accessible proof of His existence, there are few who would insist that it is irrational to assert that there is a possibility that God exists. If such is the case, then I believe that we should be passionately interested in finding out the truth of the matter. If there is evidence that may warrant rational belief in God, we should spend much time and effort in examining it, for, if God does exist, coming to knowledge of Him is the most important thing that we can do with our time. After all, the fate of our very souls would depend upon it.[28]

---

[26] Van Steenberg, *Hidden God, How Do We Know that God Exists?*, 1966.

[27] Moser, *Cognitive Idolatry and Divine Hiding* , 2002. p. 135.

[28] We shall see that this point is perhaps the most significant free action that we can initiate in the process of coming to know God, loving Him for the correct reasons, and thereby moving towards our salvation.

3

Epistemology

Why is it that certain individuals will interpret the appearance of a sign as miraculous, while another will insist that it is nothing more than a natural anomaly? The difference lies in the particular epistemologies being utilised by the different individuals when analysing the same occurrence. This sounds complicated, but it is important to remember that often an individual is unaware as to how he would philosophically render the facts that validate his particular way of looking at the world. Epistemologies usually initially occur in an unreflective way, as the products of various cultural factors (but we shall see that we can initiate a process that may allow us to adopt new epistemic standards). We interpret the world according to certain rules that we employ when faced with circumstances of particular types. This allows us to make judgements as to the nature of states of affairs and their origin. What is important is that the individual feels that he is justified in the way that he interprets the world, and is convinced that he is not being irrational or negligent in his assessment.

When we look at the world we attempt to gain meaning from/through the things that we observe, and we use our epistemological standards as a means of finding the truth and avoiding error. If we are of a religious persuasion, this meaning will be of a specific sort, whereas, if we are atheists, the same facts may be interpreted in a radically different way. When we attempt to convert those who have epistemological standards that conflict with ours, we are essentially attempting to persuade them to adopt a similar mode of interpreting the world. However, misunderstanding and conflict arise when we imagine that by listing the reasons for our beliefs we can show someone with a conflicting epistemology that he is mistaken. This is because we are failing to appreciate that the very foundation of our process of evidence-evaluation and the inferences that we make from it are not accepted as valid by our rival. This leads to what I will call an 'epistemological incommunicability'.

When the atheist and the theist approach a 'sign' (hereafter when I refer to a sign I am intending some state of affairs that *could* be interpreted as a miracle) they are in fact using the same sensory apparatus and observing the same actual state of affairs. It is not that the external world of sensory experience deviates from one person to the next – it is rather that the mode of interpreting that external world is at variance.

The world is capable of coherent and consistent understanding on either naturalistic or theistic grounds, yet some people find that they cannot but help interpret the world as mediating a divine-human encounter.[29]

Empirically observable states of affairs are not the criteria that will determine which interpretation is veridical.[30] This is because, as I have already asserted, what is actually occurring is a different interpretational reaction to the same set of observable facts. From this we can conclude that the external world will not offer us a means of validating either the truth-claim that God is evident in nature, or that God is not evident in nature.

Wisdom gives us an account of two men who have different ways of interpreting the meaning of a garden, and of a somewhat mystical gardener who may or may not have given it the appearance that it has:

Our two gardeners even when they had reached the stage when neither expected any experiential result which the other did not, might yet have continued the dispute, each presenting and representing the features of the garden favouring His hypothesis, that is, fitting His model for describing the accepted fact; each emphasizing the pattern he wishes to emphasize.[31]

His point is that people with conflicting epistemic standards view the universe entirely differently. If we believe in God, it is not just that *some* things about our world are different to that of the non-believer – it is rather that the *whole meaning* of the world is distinct.

However, from our present stand-point within the universe, this difference does not involve a difference in the objective content of each or even any of its passing moments.[32]

---

[29] Mesle, *Does God Hide from Us?*, 1988.
[30] Wisdom, *Philosophy and Psychoanalysis*, 1953, pp. 154-155.
[31] Wisdom, *Philosophy and Psychoanalysis*, 1953, p. 159.
[32] Hick, *Philosophy of Religion*, 1973.

For this reason, we can continue to interact with individuals who do not adopt our epistemic standards in meaningful ways. We can speak of the various empirical states of affairs that may or may not pertain, we can gossip, talk about the news and so forth, without there being significant problems in communicability and understanding. Where the real problem surfaces is when we speak of the meaning *behind* these various things. This is where the true difficulty in understanding and communication becomes overtly tangible.

Hare has argued that there are unverifiable interpretations of experience that cannot be falsified. He has called this phenomenon a *blik*.[33] In philosophy, we have no framework that allows us to determine with certainty which interpretation of reality is correct in any given situation. The very nature of experience, as I have already noted, is open to various interpretations; none of which are necessarily imposed on us (i.e. although I may have no choice as to my current epistemic standards there is no reason that those standards cannot change.)

The problem remains though that if we have no universally valid framework from which to proceed, it appears that there is no way for an objective investigator to decide which epistemology to adopt.[34] Mesle sums this up as follows:

> For if someone really affirms that all of these different positions can be equally compelling to an intelligent and honest seeker, it seems that none of them is really warranted.[35]

The impartial investigator will invariably find that different people have experiences that, *for them,* amount to evidence that their way of looking at the world is correct. Kvanvig notes that

> ...for almost any set of beliefs, there is some belief system in which

---

[33] Hare, *New Essays in Philosophical Theology*, 1955, P. 100.
[34] I am not suggesting here that we can ever be neutral and unbiased regarding epistemic standards in any way other than as an abstract thought-experiment.
[35] Mesle, *Does God Hide from Us?*, 1988, p. 101.

those beliefs would have good subjective epistemic standing.[36]

This is true if we allow the following rule to stand – *k* is justified in believing some proposition *p* at time *t* if there is nothing contrary to *k's* epistemic duty in believing *p* at *t*.[37]

It is important to emphasise the fact that although there may be difficulty in attempting to prescribe which world-view we should adopt, that does not mean that there is not one *correct* world-view. Therefore, it may be possible that a certain manifestation of a sign *is in fact* a supernatural occurrence. However, as Rowe points out

> ...unless the subject experiences that object as supernatural, the subject has not had a religious experience.[38]

Even if God were to appear to an individual in the guise of a burning bush and spoke to Him, unless that person had an epistemology that allowed for an experience to be acknowledged as religious, or he were prone to be swayed by such an occurrence, there would be nothing irrational in his contending that the experience was no more than an hallucination, or some other equally plausible explanation that is coherent with his world-view. Some would even contend that he would have an epistemic duty to reach such a conclusion. Once again, this calls to mind the futility of calling for God to manifest an empirically observable sign. A religious sign will only ever be a religious sign for an individual if he is open to faith *before* the occurrence.

Why can God not just make us inherently aware of His existence by way of instinct or some similar psychological state? If we had an immediate awareness, or absolute intuition of his existence, the need for an external proof or demonstration would be gratuitous. I would suggest that God does not do so because this would radically alter our mode of interaction with Him. I will argue that God does not impose the fact of His existence on us in such a fashion because he deems it important that we be

---

[36] Kvanvig, *Divine Hiddenness: What is the Problem?*, 2002. P. 150.
[37] For a fuller discussion see Schellenberg 2002.
[38] Rowe, *The Problem of Evil and Some Varieties of Atheism*, 1982. p. 23.

capable of allowing Him to pass by us unnoticed or ignored, and that He has reasons for doing so. I will return to this issue, but first I would like to consider the rationality of believing in God.

4

Rationality

Often when we profess a belief we are questioned as to its coherence and rationality. What exactly does it mean to e say that a belief should be rational? There are many different ways in which we can say that a claim is rational. However, there are two forms of rationality that are particularly relevant to the discussion at hand. What I will call 'prudential rationality' pertains to what it is prudent to believe; what will lead to actions that are wise and practical in some sense. And what I will call 'epistemic rationality' concerns how much epistemic license we legitimately have in the formation of a belief and our adherence to it. In other words, given the way in which our knowledge is structured and the rules that are embedded in our epistemic standard, does the formation of a new belief have rational justification?

Experience does not reveal itself through logical demonstration and, as such, must be known through interpretation and inference. We will often have some degree of doubt about the veracity of our interpretations of various states of affairs; as doubt in such an interpretational process cannot always be eliminated through a process of reasoning. As has been shown by Descartes, we can even doubt the very faculties that allow us to reason. I have so far shown that there is epistemic rationality in upholding the view that God exists; now it is beneficial to determine whether it is also prudentially rational. Therefore, I will ask 'is it prudent to believe that God exists?'

In offering a solution to the above question perhaps we should entertain the idea that the reflective theist is attempting to be prudent when adopting his world-view. If his understanding of the grounding of reality does not rely on certain proofs, and is instead a matter of perspectival interpretation, then perhaps our theist is of the opinion that, given the range and nature of his experience, an inferential move to the existence of God is the most probable explanation of the world as a whole, and that the evidence under consideration points towards this fact.[39] In this instance, we could think our theist as a variety of probabilist (although this obviously does not do justice to theists as a whole. For, as I have already suggested, some theists are convinced that they know with certainty that God exists, and therefore would assert that there is no element of probability involved). There is nothing epistemically irrational in this move, and it may also be seen as prudentially rational. It is prudent

---

[39] See Moser, *Cognitive Idolatry and Divine Hiding*, 2002, p. 121.

of the theist to adopt the world-view that appears to him to offer the most comprehensive explanation of the world that he encounters. It is his encounter with the world that gives rise to the conviction that God exists. In this way, God's existence becomes more than an abstract hypothesis and starts to have significance in the life of the believer. As we shall see, a belief in God is different to many of our other beliefs, as it gives rise to particular responsibilities.

We can now claim that belief in God has a strong epistemic status – it is both rational and prudential. Rowe points to this fact when he states:

> When subjects have an experience that they take to be of x, and we know how to discover positive reasons for thinking that their experience is delusive, if such reasons do exist, then it is rational to conclude that they really do experience x unless we have some positive reasons to think their experiences are delusive.[40]

Why should we think that religious experiences are delusive? The naturalist would object that what the theist is actually experiencing is nothing more than empirical phenomena and that the inferences that he is making are superfluous and mistaken, given that the same state of affairs can be explained without resorting to the 'supernatural'.

When I see a beautiful sunset, why also propose that I see it as evidence of the existence of God? As Digby rightly notes:

> There is apparently no available (certain) knowledge to connect sunsets, etc., with God (the conceptual apparatus of theism alone being inadequate for this purpose). But, again, even if such knowledge were available, it would only support an *inference* (not 'sensory detection' of God's presence).[41]

Does such an objection provide positive reasons for supposing that religious experiences are delusive? I would suggest that such narrow naturalism fails to consider the transcendental element that such

---

[40] Rowe, *Religious Experience and the Principle of Credulity*, 1982. p. 23.
[41] Digby, *On Observability and Detectability*, 1991, p. 511.

experiences involve. When the theist experiences a sunset (or any other event, sign or occurrence) as evidence of the existence of God, he is not proposing that it is a sensory detection of God's actual presence. What he is actually describing is an awareness of a sense of order and goodness that underlies the very being of the physical phenomenon in question. He would not argue that *physically* the sunset is anything more than a product of the rotation of the earth in relation to the sun and so forth, but he would insist that it is still evidence of the divine. If there is no sufficiently convincing reason to suppose that religious experiences are delusive in this way (and I would strongly contend that there is not), then we cannot dismiss them because they seem incredible or epistemically weak to those who are strong naturalists with atheistic world-views. There is nothing *irrational* in having a religious perspective and, because of the arguments outlined above, I think that this is a fact that *everyone* should give assent to, irrespective of whether they are theists or not. To acknowledge that something is a rational possibility is not, after all, the same as attaching significant epistemic weight to it in one's *own* view.

The problem that we still have is that, although we have epistemic warrant to hold that there is a God, this claim is no more forceful to the objective investigator than the claim that there is no God. For now I would draw attention to Moser's formulation of the problem:

> The true God would not settle for thin theism but would promote cognitively robust theism: the view that we epistemically should lovingly believe in, or trust, God as the Lord of our lives. Cognitively robust theism entails cognitively thin theism but requires a life-commitment to a personal Lord, beyond rational belief that God exists. This Lord is not the conclusion of an argument but is rather the personal enabler of any person offering an argument.[42]

For the religious believer, it should not be important for him to be able to formulate his beliefs such that they can be universally validated, this is a snare that many apologists have fallen into. Numerous beliefs are unfalsifiable – they are what I have already alluded to as *bliks*. As such, we cannot definitively say if they are true or false outside of the epistemology

---

[42] Moser, *Cognitive Idolatry and Divine Hiding*, 2002, pp. 125-126.

of the believer. But that is not to say that the believer cannot have knowledge of them as true or false – because of the epistemology that he has adopted (which *may* be correct), and because of the private experiences that have led him to adopt these beliefs (which *may* be true). Just because I cannot prove that God exists because of a sunset, that does not mean that I do not see evidence of God in the sunset, or that such evidence leads to true knowledge. It may be an inference, but true knowledge may be gained as the result of that inference.

Many propositions may be true, despite the fact that we have no way of validating their premises. Hare, however, makes an important point when he says that we need to differentiate between *right* and *wrong bliks*.[43] There are many things that are unfalsifiable, for instance, solipsism – but that does not mean that I will want to base my whole mode of interacting with the things that I experience on this fact. I may therefore be justified in calling these *wrong bliks*. To this end, the religious believer should be able to provide positive reasons for the beliefs that he holds. The individual has a responsibility to seriously consider whether the unfalsifiable beliefs that he allows into His world-view are actually representative of the way that the world *really is*. He should reflective consider the reasons that form the foundation of his beliefs. After all, the theist, as much as anyone else, should not want to be subject to illusory fabrications.

---

[43]Hare, *New Essays in Philosophical Theology*, 1955, p. 100.

5

Freedom and Conversion

For us to be free autonomous religious believers it is important that we are rationally free in a significant sense. Many commentators on the Christian God find it important that we should be able to come to a free rational decision to believe in Him and dedicate ourselves to Him. This must be a free decision unencumbered by any coercive influence (although in the history of the Bible there have been individuals that God has chosen to exempt from this provision).

If we are all exposed to the same observable facts and if we do not, or can not, see God at work in the universe, is the fault with us or is it a fault in the constitution that we were provided with by God? If we are not free to change our epistemic standards then surely we cannot be held responsible for not believing in God if we are strong naturalists.

I would now like to explore the idea that we can effect a conversion to theism through a freely initiated process. Michael Dummet states:

> God is just and cannot wish or require anyone to believe that which there is no reason to believe.[44]

We have already seen that the theist's to beliefs concerning the existence of God are rational, but we must also remember that the Judeo-Christian God demands that *all* men believe in Him. It appears that a loving God could not make a demand of man that he is unable to achieve. So it seems that all men should be able to accomplish a theistic conversion. I have shown that even the sceptic should admit to the *possibility* of there being a God. However, I have also shown that an individual has an epistemic duty to search for the truth within the parameters of his own epistemological framework, unless that framework is shown to have fault. For example, a naturalist appears to have an epistemic duty to search for truth based on his particular world-view that all things have a natural explanation. There are two questions that we must therefore proceed to ask – (i) can this person reach a state of spiritual awakening such that a conversion is appropriate, and (ii) should this person attempt to nourish the conditions that would allow such a conversion to occur?

---

[44] Dummett, in Stump and Flint, *Hermes and Athena: Biblical Exegesis and Philosophical Theology*, 1993.

Pascal answers our first question by insisting that one can freely and intentionally bring oneself to a conversion.

> You would like to attain faith, and do not know the way, you would like to cure yourself of unbelief, and ask the remedy for it. Learn of those who have been bound like you…Follow the way by which the began; by acting as if they believed, taking the holy water, having masses said etc. Even this will naturally make you believe and decide your acuteness.[45]

Pascal's remedy is to learn from those who have had a similar experience and *act as though* you are already a practicing Christian theist. However, we must note that even Pascal was aware of the fact that for any conversion to occur there must be an interest present in the sceptic, such that he recognises that the fruits of conversion are worth the pursuit. Is this argument sufficient to convince the atheist? It appears that it will only be successfully agreed upon by someone who has already accepted the idea that it is possibly better to be a theist than an atheist. Why would one reach this conclusion?

John Hick believes that the ambiguity of the world, the very fact that it can be interpreted either naturalistically or theistically, is a divine test through which the worthy are separated from the unworthy. Those who pass come to knowledge of the divine, despite the fact that the evidence does not necessarily conclusively prove God's existence. Yet there is something a little unsettling about this account. How can we pass a test when the cards seem to be stacked against us from the outset? We have already seen that, if there is even the remotest chance that God exists, we should take great interest in the fact, because the greatest of stakes, our souls, are at risk (it can be argued that even if you do not currently believe in the existence of the soul, you should be interested in the fact that the soul *might* exist, and for this reason do everything in your power to find the truth of the matter). God should, therefore, become our ultimate concern, at least until we can definitively decide that He does not exist, having attempted to use all means at our disposal to find Him.

---

[45] Pascal, Pensees, No. 233, p. 68, trans. found in Hick 1973. p. 54.

"God"…is the name for that which concerns man ultimately. This does not mean that first there is a being called God and then the demand that man should be ultimately concerned about Him. It means that whatever concerns a man ultimately becomes God for Him, and, conversely, it means that a man can be concerned ultimately only about that which is god for Him.[46]

If man should be ultimately concerned with divinity and the fate of the soul, then he should be careful to try to find the God that can address his concerns. Man can put faith in God, or he can alternatively put faith in the figments of his own imagination and make them into his God. Nevertheless, the venture of attempting to find God should be earnestly pursued. After all, what have we lost if at the end of the attempt we still do not believe? We have retained our initial beliefs and possibly given them a stronger foundation. It is well to note that from the naturalistic viewpoint there can be no guarantee that trying to find God will bear any fruit, and the greatest likelihood that it will not. That does not mean though that for this reason the endeavour should be abandoned or scorned. Tennant makes this point when he says

Hopeful experimenting has not produced the machine capable of perpetual motion; and had Columbus steered with confidence for Utopia he would not have found it.[47]

But he proceeds to qualify,

Belief is more or less constrained by fact of Actuality that already is or will be, independently of any striving of ours, and which convinces us. Faith, on the other hand, reaches beyond the Actual or the given to the ideally possible, which in the first instance it creates, as the mathematician posits His entities, and then by practical activity may realise or bring into Actuality. Every

---

[46] Tillich, *Systematic Theology*, I, 1951. p. 59. I am going farther in my extrapolation of the consequences of this statement than I think Tillich intended.

[47] Tennant, 1930, *Philosophical Theology*, I, p. 297.

machine of human invention has thus come to be. Again, faith may similarly lead to knowledge of Actuality which it in no sense creates, but which would have continued, in absence of the faith-venture, to be unknown: as in the discovery of America by Columbus.[48]

Thus, we see that although belief may be dependent on conditions that are beyond the scope of our control, we have it in our power to try to believe – to have faith, or, more accurately, to begin the process of faith. Through faith it may be possible to come to belief, to come to knowledge of those things that are currently beyond our grasp, because of our epistemological constraints. In all great ventures there is a degree of faith in the outcome, and it is this faith that is essential to religious conversion. It is both epistemically rational to make the attempt and prudentially rational to try to come to knowledge of God, as if our souls are eternal, then their care and improvement must be of ultimate concern, as must the principle that sustains them (once again I would stress it is prudent to pursue God even on the chance that this is the case).

I have been talking a great deal of 'ultimate concern' – but what exactly do I mean by this phrase? Tillich formulates his definition of ultimate concern as follows:

> Ultimate concern is the abstract translation of the great commandment: "The Lord, our God, the Lord is one; and you shall love the Lord your God with all your heart, and with all your soul, and with all your mind, and with all your strength." The religious concern is ultimate; it excludes all other concerns from ultimate significance; it makes them preliminary. The ultimate concern is unconditional, independent of any conditions of character, desire, or circumstance. The unconditional concern is total: no part of ourselves or of our world is excluded from it; there is no "place" to flee from it. The total concern is infinite: no moment of relaxation and rest is possible in the face of a religious concern which is ultimate, unconditional, total, and infinite.[49]

---

[48] Ibid.
[49] Tillich, *Systematic Theology I*, 1951, I, 11-12.

I would propose that this is ultimate concern at its highest and most refined. This is not immediately possible however for the atheist that attempts to come to know God, for although he may seriously love the idea of an ultimate grounding of reality that is the supreme instance of goodness and love, this is substantially different from loving the actual supreme personification of these characteristics, and having belief in the existence of such a being. The love that we offer to something we think is fictional and the love that we offer to another person are of a different order (although I do not deny that both can be felt quite strongly). What I think should initially be of ultimate concern to the atheist is the fact that such an entity *could* exist, and through the process of faith, following prescriptions somewhat similar to those suggested by Pascal (although I do not suggest his exact proscriptions), it may be possible to come to knowledge of God. If faith is followed by belief, then it may be possible for the potential convertee to eventually adopt Tennant's formulation of ultimate concern, and possibly to act on it. I would further propose that the atheist's awareness of the possibility of God should sufficiently warrant the postponement of his adherence to a naturalistic world-view, at least for a time.

> If we can intentionally begin the process of faith and hope that this turns to belief (or at least accept that it might) then we must ask what happens that allows the change from faith to belief, the shift that changes the onus of our ultimate concern? Newman offers us the idea of a 'threshold' concept. A belief is not something that occurs in a vacuum, it is the culmination of a process, and once that process is complete and the belief is integrated into the individuals world-view then its integrity may require that other beliefs be surrendered. This surrendering of other beliefs may be necessary to sustain the integrity of the world-view that has been newly adopted or modified. In Newman's language, once we have integrated a new belief we have given it *assent*. Assent is all or nothing. At the utmost we say that we are inclined to believe this proposition or that, that we are not sure it is not true, that much may be said for it, that we have been struck by it; but we never say that we give it a degree of assent. We might as well talk of degrees

of truth as degrees of assent.[50]

What is known as the 'threshold' view proposes that once we have passed the critical threshold of a development then it is complete. Once water boils its substantive transition is finished, it does not allow of degrees – either it is boiling or it is not. But is the above idea based on an underlying ambiguity? Even theists admit that there are different degrees of faith. If one believes in God and yet does not have a strong faith, how can this be the case? Newman offers the following answer:

> [an] increase or decrease of strength does not lie in the assent itself, but in its circumstances and concomitants; for instance, in the emotions, in the rationcinative faculty, or in the imagination...Such strength is adventitious and accidental; it may come, it may go...it does not interfere with the genuineness and perfection of the act of assent."[51]

It is my contention that we are not free to form beliefs by intention alone, but we are free to begin a process of faith that may eventually lead to belief. We do in fact have a duty to make this attempt, and the very fact that we can refuse to do so is what lends moral significance to our decision. God has let us know that he *may* exist – and this alone should be sufficient for us to try to come to know Him (it is obvious that not all men are introduced to the idea of monotheism, or at least in the past have not been).

---

[50] Newman 1870, ed. Kerr, 1985, p. 174.
[51] Ibid. p. 184-185.

6
Coercion

It seems that, despite all that has been so far discussed, a satisfactory answer has still not been provided as to why God does not reveal Himself to all of mankind in an unambiguous fashion. There is a school of thought that believes that any such manifestation would obliterate human freedom. Some philosophers have reached the conclusion that it would be impossible to have a direct and unmistakable encounter with the divine, and retain an unaffected free will. For the believer, God is not just an abstract idea – He is the very grounding on which reality is founded, and the principle that sustains the created world. If we come to know Him, we come to know Him as the entity that permits our very being, and allows us to be who we are and do what we do. We would instantly become aware that we have a teleological purpose that is inextricably bound to the divine will. It can then be argued that our ultimate goal would inevitably be to please God, and so ensure the continuation of our soul and a favourable judgement at the end of days. All other concerns would significantly diminish, as nothing else could exert the same influence over our lives and our decision making process. This influence would have to be coercive, and so detrimental to our status as free autonomous agents. Hick conforms to this view when he writes:

> Therefore it is said, God does not present Himself to us as a reality of the same order as ourselves. If he were to do so, the finite being would be swallowed by the infinite Being.[52]

Put in simple terms, we would not be able to preserve ourselves as free agents if we were to come to an immediate certainty of the existence of God (In pursuing this line of reasoning, one would have to also assert that for this reason we are different from angels and demons. Angels are aware of the existence of God and yet act freely and demons have been cast out precisely because they freely rebelled against divine decree). For this reason, there must be a process of approaching the divine that allows us to retain our freedom and autonomy.

How is this possible? God creates us at an epistemic distance that is sufficient to protect us, and yet is not so distant as to prevent a gradual

---

[52] Hick, *Philosophy of Religion*, 1973.

approach. The hiddenness of God, thought of in this light, is conducive to the preservation of man's individuality and a process of spiritual evolution that will eventually culminate in belief. Pascal believes that God does not wish to overwhelm our faculties and so, instead of giving us cognitive certainty, offers to help to transform our will.

> God wishes to move the will rather than the mind...Perfect clarity would help the mind and harm the will.[53]

Accordingly, it appears that if the atheist was given the irrefutable evidence that he demands, he would have to pay a terrible cost. Hick lucidly sums up the whole position when he states:

> God's self-revealing actions are accordingly always so mediated through the events composing our temporal experience that men only become aware of the divine presence by interpreting and responding to these events in the way which we call religious faith. For if God were to disclose Himself to us in the coercive manner in which our physical environment obtrudes itself we should be dwarfed to nothingness by the infinite power thus irresistibly breaking open the privacy of our souls. Further, we should be spiritually bounded by God's perfect holiness and paralyzed by His infinite energy; for "human kind cannot bear very much reality." (T. S. Eliot, "Burnt Norton," I, Four Quartets (London: Faber &Faber, 1944)."[54]

It is fair to state that if a man recognised that a sign from God provided irrefutable evidence that He exists, it would be irrational for him to deny the existence of God. It follows from the above argument that this would destroy the individual's freedom for various reasons. But this second claim is not uncontroversial. Penelhum refutes it when he points out that for any proposition *p* that has sound premises, an individual can recognise

---

[53] Pascal, Pensees, Fragment, 234, in Schelleberg, *Divine Hiddenness and Human Reason*, 1993, p. 135.
[54] Hick, *The Existence of God*, 1964, p. 16.

the logical validity of *p* and still reject it.

> [Facts] which proved [the] …existence [of God]…where this is
> understood to mean merely that they entailed it or made it
> overwhelmingly probable, so that disbelief was thereby shown to
> be irrational…do not compel assent…because men are irrational
> and do deceive themselves.[55]

According to Penelhum's argument, we could be given proof that God
exists and yet still fail to believe in Him, and could thereby retain our
freedom even in the face of conclusive evidence. It can accordingly be
argued that a certain disclosure of God does not necessarily entail that all
its recipients would be coerced. This argument presupposes that, in the
case of a certain disclosure of the existence of God, we would be coerced
into certain activities, and is only a valid as long as we accept that man can
be cognitively negligent and has some sort of control over the process of
cognitive negligence. Nevertheless, it should be noted that when we are
cognitively negligent it may be possible for others to force assent to the
correct conclusion through demonstration and correct argumentation. We
are not talking here about different epistemic points of view – if we are
given conclusive proof and are certain that a certain state of affairs obtains,
we have *knowledge* of this fact and do not merely hold an opinion about it.
Once we have been shown that we are being cognitively negligent it
would be irrational for us to maintain our previous stance (the whole
point of my earlier discussion of epistemology was to show that neither
the naturalistic or theistic stances were cognitively negligent).

The only way it appears that Penelhum's argument would hold is if we
were in permanent isolation, or permanently kept the exclusive company
of a group of similarly cognitively negligent individuals, for if we were
exposed to those holding the correct point of view then we would
inevitably have to change our opinion, or at the very least admit the
irrationality of our perspective – which would seriously undermine it. We
might refuse to allow ourselves to consider the question when in the
presence of others not of our opinion – but this would show at least a

---

[55] This abbreviated version is found in McKim, *The Hiddenness of God*, 1990, and is taken
from Penelhum's *Problems of Religious Knowledge*.

subconscious awareness that our opinion is in some way deficient. We might fool ourselves but we would know at a significant level that we are intentionally fooling ourselves. Thus, Penelhum's argument does not hold much weight given the difficulty of maintaining the position that he discusses, although we must allow that in very specific conditions it is a possibility.

How then would we be coerced by evidence of God? The coercion in question cannot be physical, as no facts about the material world would have changed. For some there would be a radical epistemological shift in accepting a belief of this magnitude. The options that we are left with are those of cognitive or psychological compulsion. What form would this take? I will deal with the latter first. The psychological compulsion in question is not that of insanity for there is nothing insane in recognising an irrefutable proof as an irrefutable proof, furthermore, there is no evidence to suggest that insanity would result as a consequence of belief in God. What it seems we are talking about then is the psychological compulsion involved in threat situations. In what I will call a *divine threat situation* there is no physical reason why a certain act cannot be performed. Nor does there seem to be any metaphysical reason as to why it would be impossible to choose from a variety of alternative actions when one feels threatened.

In offering an account of the type of coercion that a divine threat situation instantiates let us consider the nature of the threat itself. Schellenberg sums up the situation thus:

> Considering themselves to be observed by the all-seeing eye of God, human beings would do only what they considered God's will, out of fear of divine wrath.[56]

I take this to be referring to a fear of judgement and sentence at the end of time.

Is it true that we can ever be threatened to such a degree that we become powerless to act contrary to the demands of the threatener, or contrary to what we believe to be his desire? As we have seen above, in

---

[56] Schellenberg, *What the Hiddenness of God Reveals*, 2002, p. 25.

this context there are several types of freedom to be considered. Murray proposes that if faced with a significant threat we may find it irrational to choose other than a single action in response.[57] The consequences of acting otherwise would carry sufficient epistemic weight to stifle any inclination to do so. If we perceive a threatening situation to be of such magnitude that we cannot but comply with the threatener, then we have no real freedom in our choice formation. Howard-Snyder claims that this is the reason that God does not give us a full disclosure of His existence.[58] Such a state of affairs would ensure that the approach to God was based on the wrong motivations – such as fear of being punished. As long as there is some doubt about the existence of God the epistemic force of the threat is diminished.

However, neither of these claims is self-apparent. It is impossible to show that any threat situation is such that it is impossible to initiate more than a single action. To say that it is irrational to do other than the threatener wishes is also not self-apparent, in the context of divine disclosure. After all, when the angels rebelled against God one could not say that their actions were irrational – they had perfectly good reasons for their actions and were capable of giving an account of them. To act from pride is not irrational, if one believes that one's pride should be given greater weight than obedience to the divine, even if one knows that there will be consequences of a certain type, as the rebellious angels did. One could not claim that Adam's sin was irrational. It was morally wanting, but not irrational – again he could provide perfectly good reasons for his actions, even though he knew that he would incur the wrath of God.

So then, what of Murray's claim that:

> what is not possible in these threat contexts, are free actions that are morally significant?[59]

Many philosophers agree that we cannot be held responsible for acts that are performed under compulsion.[60] However, I have already shown

---

[57] Murray, *Deus Absconditus*, 2002, p. 30.
[58] Howard-Snyder, *Introduction, The Hiddenness of God*, 2002, p. 9.
[59] Murray, *Deus Absconditus* , 2002, p. 30.
[60] Tipton, *The Handbook of Western Philosophy*, 1988, p. 500.

the flaw in Murray's argument - there is no sufficient reason to suppose that any threat situation is such that our response to it is compulsive. It is hard to imagine a threat situation with greater force than torture and execution, such as was done to martyrs in various eras and under various regimes. If it was possible for some to resist the force of such a threat, then it may be *possible* for all to do so. Furthermore, the demons (of Christian belief) are sure of the existence of God and yet act in defiance of Him. And once again the fallen angels knew what their fate would be if they rebelled against God the omnipotent creator of all, and yet they did so out of lust for power and vanity. Even if we read this as an allegory, we can still appreciate its applicability to the question at hand. Even if we are certain that an act will result in horrendous consequences for us, there may be various reasons that permit us to make the choice to consign ourselves to those consequences.

Now I will proceed to the question of cognitive freedom and the effects of a divine disclosure. In most things that men observe, they do not have cognitive freedom to decide whether or not they do in fact exist – the disclosure that is the result of an observation is itself sufficient to determine its existence for the observer. For example, in common observation, when I see a tree, I do not instigate a cognitive process through which I come to choose whether or not to believe that there is in fact a tree in existence, whose form I perceive. The world in this way forces itself upon me. It is also appropriate that I respond in this way – if I did not, it would be impossible for me to interact with the things in my environment successfully. When I observe an aspect of my environment, unless I have reasons to doubt the veracity of my senses for various reasons (such as insanity, being under the influence of drugs and so forth), I automatically proceed to take the existence of the thing observed for granted. Is it true then that it is important that I be able to come to a cognitively free choice to believe in God's existence?

If God were to give us a certain disclosure of His existence then it is true that we would not have a free cognitive choice to believe in Him – but why would this be a negative thing? I do not think that the arguments presented in the previous discussion have been compelling enough to prevent us from looking for more convincing reasons for divine hiddenness.

.

7

A Personal Relationship

Schellenberg suggests that we should not assume that God wants His existence to remain hidden or obscure.[61] Because of the nature of God, the personification of pure love,[62] he must desire that we come to know Him and thereby enter into a relationship with Him. But, as in all mutually loving personal relationships, the love involved has a reciprocal character that requires the interaction and application of both parties. However, God's original plan was that the acknowledgement of, and openness to, the divine must come from us.[63]

Why is it that for a meaningful relationship with God He must remain cognitively distanced from us, if, as we have seen, such a disclosure would still leave room for significant free moral action? What are the conditions that necessitate such a state of affairs? Hick writes:

> The reason why God reveals Himself indirectly – meeting us in and through the world as mediating a significance that requires an appropriate response on our part… is that only thus can the conditions exist for a personal relationship between God and man.[64]

What are these conditions for the Christian? We must come to know God in a fashion that will allow for spiritual growth and moral evolution, without being detrimental to our free will. We must come to love God as *our* God, because He is the ultimate foundation of all that exists, of all that is good in this world and of all that is worth pursuing in the next. For the Christian, God offers His love before we ever approach Him; it is an open invitation that only needs to be accepted by us. Our response to the invitation must be free – for what could it possibly mean to love someone if that love were not freely offered and could not be freely accepted or refused?

Love derives its value, at least in part, from that fact that the way we respond to it is at our discretion. I am not suggesting that we can always

---

[61] Schellenberg, *Divine Hiddenness and Human Reason*, 1993.

[62] "Love – real love – is one of the most awesome qualities of personal being we know of (and even that may be an understatement). How could God exist but lack it? If God lacked it, God could not be unsurpassably great." Schellenberg, 2002, p. 41.

[63] Ross, *The Hiddenness of God, A Puzzle or a Real Problem?*, 2002.

[64] Hick, *Faith and Knowledge*, 1981, p. 140.

chose to love, and sometimes we find that we still love those who have deeply hurt us, even though we would prefer to have no feelings towards them whatsoever. But God is different from man in the fact that He is *love itself*; He always offers love and the love that He offers is of the purest sort. The same is not true of man. Man can choose to ignore the invitation to love or to scorn it.

> God hides and thus permits ...nonbelief because, if He were not hidden, humans would relate to God and to their knowledge of God in presumptuous ways and the possibility of developing the inner attitudes essential to a proper relationship with Him would be *ipso facto* ruled out."[65]

Our motivation in our approach to God is of great significance, and decides whether or not we will be able to recognise the offer of love that He makes to us. God would not coerce or necessitate a particular approach, for if He did the value of the entire undertaking would be obliterated. As Gerrish claims:

> ...genuine love presupposes freedom, since love is a free gift of oneself to another, any psychological states causally necessitated in a person by someone else would not count as love. If love requires human freedom, then, it is logically impossible for God to bring about the salvation of anyone who refuses to love Him.[66]

If we cannot always choose who we love, then the freedom that makes the love valuable is not located in the volitional decision to love, for such a decision is in fact never made. Where there is value is in the *response* that we choose to make to the love that we encounter; in the actual reciprocal *offering* of our love or in the *attempt* to return the emotion. We can refuse love, resent it, suppress it or embrace it.

If we choose to embrace love, then we are intentionally placing ourselves in a position in which it may be possible for us to come to love

[65] Howard-Snyder, *Introduction, The Hiddenness of God,* 2002, p. 10.

[66] Gerrish, *"To the Unkown God": Luther and Calvin on the Hiddenness of God,* 1973, p. 84.

the other (presuming that we do not already do so). Love requires a substantive shift – it cannot be forced – there are many people that we would choose to love if we could, but for whom we cannot find the resources within ourselves.

What I propose, therefore, is that the freedom that is essential to a human response to divine love is the freedom to form, or refuse to form, an *appropriate response*. The realisation that the ultimate Good loves us will not crush our ability to react to this love with scorn or indifference, for such is the fickle nature of man. Even the Bible does not suggest that we can make ourselves love if our inclination is to the contrary. If we were to realise that the love that we have for God has been causally necessitated by Him, then we may do as the fallen-angels did and resent it, providing we still retained the freedom to form a reactive attitude. For this reason, Lev. 19:18, 34 commands an *act* of love and not love itself.[67] An act of love is forming a morally appropriate response to those that we encounter. Therefore, the love that God offers us requires an appropriate moral response. Generally, it is in man's nature to love that which is in his best interests, and loving God is always in the best interest of man.

The God of Love loves that which he has created, for all created things are good. To impose the divine will on the created will of man would radically alter the divine- human relationship. It is because of this fact that God leaves it entirely up to us to embrace or reject Him.[68] If we take the time to be passionately interested, we will come to know and embrace the love of God, but if we refuse for any one of a myriad of possible reasons then God will take no further steps to ensure that we spiritually progress.

> Belief in God is normally more than a cognitive matter, and our volitional stance, (especially our attitudes) may be such that God may not give us more knowledge of Himself until we turn toward Him with greater interest and openness.[69]

The path to salvation is laid open at our feet and it is up to us to take the first faltering steps. Once we have accomplished this much, the love of

---

[67] Pointed out by McKim, *The Hiddenness of God*, 1990, p. 57.

[68] See for Example Howard-Snyder 1996, *The Argument from Divine Hiddenness*, p. 434.

[69] Garcia, *St. John of the Cross and the Necessity of Divine Hiddenness*, 2002. p. 86.

God will help us on our way. Because of this fact, we must accept some degree of culpability for not finding God if we fail to be passionately interested in doing so. God is supremely interested in relating to us, but we should not expect Him to do all the work for us, especially if the only way open for Him to force a conversion is by obliterating our will or compromising our freedom – He will not make us love Him.

> The best lover will not disclose herself to the beloved at time *t* if she can see in doing so that she would likely produce a harm that could not be sufficiently ameliorated or absorbed in the beloved's life as a whole , *or* that in doing so she would likely prevent personal relationship for a significant period beginning at *t* or some time after *t*.[70]

I would once again stress that just because a man seeks God, that does not meant that he seeks Him for the right reasons. I have already shown that a man may seek God by becoming passionately interested in finding Him. In the account that I offered it may have appeared that some of the motivation involved was selfish and aimed at self-preservation. Perhaps this is the case, but God has made man such that he must pursue his own good and the ultimate good of man, if he is capable of realising it, is God. The point that I would put is that this interestedness in the origin of the created world and the meaning of it, including man, his life and works, and also the yearning for eternal life, may eventually evolve into a love of God *as* God, and not as the means to an end. According to theists, we should not love God merely because he promises rewards to the faithful, we should attempt to distance ourselves from the selfishness of such a desire and instead love the divine because of its perfection.

Van Inwagen rightly asserts:

> …the proposition: *God wants people to believe in His existence* does not entail the proposition: *God wants people to believe in His existence and He does not care why anyone who believes in Him has this belief*.[71]

---

[70] Character S speaking in Schellenberg, *What the Hiddenness of God Reveals*, 2002, p. 49.
[71] Van Inwagen, *What is the Problem of the Hiddenness of God?*, 2002, p. 31.

Man is capable of loving many things, himself included, and so we need to add the qualification that it is not sufficient that man attempt to love God, once more we must add 'in appropriate way' – that is, as an end in itself and not as the means to the satisfaction of a personal end. The love that we offer God cannot be deficient, as such deficiency prevents the divine disclosure that is sought. If love involves a substantive change, then the love that we reciprocate to God must be of a caliber befitting its object (or as close as is humanly possible). We may be powerless over the love that we form, but we are not powerless over the love that we attempt to form. If initially we approach God for the wrong reasons, it is still within our power to reflect on this fact and attempt to remedy the situation. If the only way we can come to attempt to know God is from a selfish motivation, this is not necessarily the beginning of an evil process, as long as at some juncture we come to love God Himself. The way that God helps this to occur will be dealt with below.

8
Cognitive Freedom

The question that we must now address is whether a certain disclosure of the existence of God would rob man of significant freedom. It is obvious that if we had a certain disclosure of God we would no longer be free to reach a conclusion as to whether or not we would chose to conform to the belief that he exists. In this sense, we would not be cognitively free to accept or reject the proposition "God exists", because it would be undeniably apparent. But this in itself would not really be a significant loss of freedom. We have already shown that man has no cognitive freedom about belief formation with regard to the existence of many of the everyday objects that he encounters. The more important question is whether the loss of this cognitive freedom would be detrimental to the relationship between God and man. Dilley points out that:

> …the sense of faith that matters in religion is not mere "belief *that*" God exists, but "belief in God…creatures would not be forced into "being religious" any more than Adam or Satan were.[72]

McKim concurs, when he asserts that even when a person has correctly formed beliefs about God he would still have the ability to decide whether or not those beliefs would play an important role in his life.[73]

Because of the constitution of man's psychology he has the ability to reject even that which he knows is in his best interests (consider, for example, Dostoevsky's 'underground man' in *Notes from the Underground*). A certainty about something does not necessarily mean that it will be embraced and loved, even if to do anything else was known to be detrimental to one's personal well-being in the long-run. Could certainty of the validity of the proposition "God exists" ever compel more than "notional assent" to the validity of the assertion? Newman defines the idea of 'notional assent' and 'real assent' as follows: A notional assent is nothing more than the affirmation that a proposition obtains, a real assent occurs when the notional assent is given a free response such that it is embraced and integrated into the life of the individual. [74] Not only is the proposition affirmed to be true – the content of it and the ramifications for

---

[72] Dilley, *Fool-Proof Proofs of God?*, 1977, p. 21-23.
[73] McKim, *The Hiddenness of God*, 1990.
[74] Newman, *An Essay in Aid of a Grammar of Assent*, 1879.

future belief formation are embraced. Notional assent does not have the power to force religious conversion and exert a coercive influence.[75] It does not even have substantial religious value, for unless the person who has notional assent chooses to embrace a religious way of looking at the world he will not have had a substantive religious experience.

However, although it may be true that we would not be forced to have faith in God even if we knew that he existed, it would be very difficult for most people not try to have faith for one reason or another. But even if this were the case why would it be deemed undesirable? Keller asks:

> ...why could not rational belief that God loves them motivate people to love God out of gratitude or some similar motive?[76]

The above points shows the ineffectiveness of theories such as Hick's view of coercion, for it is not at all evident that a cognitive certainty of the existence of God would mitigate the essential aspects of man's freedom in relation to the divine – namely His response to God. However, that is not to say that God is not justified in His hiddenness. Although people would not be forced to love God, it is probable that many would approach Him for the wrong reasons, and perhaps this is sufficient justification in itself. Even though many might approach with a sincere and loving heart, God might not view this as adequate grounds for revising the degree of epistemic distancing that he has established between Himself and man.

---

[75] See Hick, *The Existence of God*, 1964, p. 18.
[76] Keller, *The Hiddenness of God and the Problem of Evil*, 1995, p. 19.

9
Grace

For salvation, the Christian believes that man is in need of divine assistance in the form of grace. However, we now must address the question as to whether grace is offered to all, or whether it is reserved for the few. The Christian insists that it is God's wish that all be saved, and that this can only be achieved through faith and filial love through Jesus Christ. Yet this presents us with a difficulty, as not all men are privy to equal exposure to the Bible and Christian teaching – indeed the Christian Church is not even known to all. Why is it that God does not provide all men with an equal opportunity to know Him? Why does he seem to favour some over others? Why does God allow differing degrees of hiddenness in different cultures and in relation to different individuals?

Moser draws our attention to the fact that

> Conceivably, God hides on occasion from some people for various reasons, including, (a) to teach people to yearn for, and thus eventually to value, personal relationship with God, (b) to strengthen grateful trust in God even when times look bleak, (c) to remove human complacency towards God and God's purposes, and (d) to shatter prideful human self-reliance.[77]

These are all areas that have already been considered and, as long as we are talking about a supremely loving God, we have found (or will shortly find) reasons for justifying these ideas. However, whilst I have shown that we have a responsibility to seek out God, and that every man has the ability to form the idea of a supremely good principle grounding all experience (we must admit of the possibility, no matter how unlikely that someone in a polytheistic society can form the idea of a monotheistic God). Furthermore, the conditions conducive to such an inference are of widely varying degrees, given each individual's Historic and cultural background:

> if many creatures are in the dark about the existence and nature of the creator, then the appropriate human responses are, at least,

---

[77] Moser, *Cognitive Idolatry and Divine Hiding*, 2002, p. 132.

made more difficult than they otherwise might be…it inhibits the fulfilment of many duties.[78]

The idea of the existence of Christ cannot spontaneously emerge as the result of being passionately interested in theism. One needs to be introduced to the idea of Christianity, before one can form an appropriate attitude to Jesus. After all, it is one thing to come to belief in God and quite another to accept that a man called Jesus was both God and man, born of a virgin and so forth.

One can claim that there is evidence for the existence of God in the created world, but the evidence that one might claim for the existence of Christ is of an entirely different order. I may be able to infer the existence of a supreme foundation of all that exists, who is the ultimate principle of love and benevolence, but without introduction to the Bible, either by direct contact or mediation, I will never come to know Jesus or have an opportunity to form a filial bond with Him. This is a problem that the Christian must attempt to address. It is especially significant if we subscribe to the formulation of grace articulated by St. Augustine, whereby we can only return to God through Christ.

One of the responses intrinsic to Judaism is the idea that God has made for Himself a chosen people. This is an idea that is present in the Hebraic understanding of the Old Testament and finds precedence in Genesis (Genesis 12:3, 22:15-18, 28:13-14). From this foundation we can interpret the idea of grace as follows: God has elected a chosen few to spread among the nations, converting those that they meet and through this process eventually bringing all of mankind to knowledge of the supreme God. This notion offers a grounding for an explanation of why God allows whole nations to remain ignorant of Him for generations.[79] We should bear in mind that traditionally grace is not bestowed according to merit, but is a gratuitous gift that is offered without desert.

Following this line of thought, there is no reason why God should offer to save all of mankind, or why He should treat all men equally. Indeed, it is a sign of His supreme mercy that He permits any to be saved, and even more so that He has allowed for one Church to save all those who do not

---

[78] McKim, *The Hiddenness of God*, 1990, p. 142.

[79] This issue is raised by Howard-Snyder, *The Argument from Divine Hiddenness*, 1996, p. 452.

as of yet know of Him. In this way God places the onus for man's salvation back on man.

We have entered our current state as a *massa damnata*[80] and it is as a mass that we should once again reclaim access to the kingdom of heaven. One of God's primary commands is to love all men, and what better evidence could there be for this love than individual men setting about the conversion of others, despite the trials and hardships that will invariably result from such a mission. And so, the Christian can offer this argument as an explanation of why God allows different men and cultures to be in different epistemic situations regarding evidence for His existence and exposure to His gospels.[81]

What then of the historical prophets to whom God appeared or spoke? The Christian might argue that it was necessary that God originally confirm His existence to eye-witnesses so that their records would serve as an inspiration and attestation to events that were of great importance. But it was God's plan that later men should believe without having seen, as this is the supreme act of faith. Each Christian is to become 'Christ-like' in his actions and the example he sets, thereby showing others the truth of the gospels, and becoming models from which others can attempt to learn and grow. Wainwright points out that this is not a lamentable state of affairs:

> …each receives His or her good from another, and then bestows that good on a third, is itself a great good. But the *greatest* good we can ever give or receive is faith. Hence our (partial) dependence on others for it is also a great good.[82]

This account is obviously not uncontroversial. It seems that although there is no definite reason we can give as to why God has any obligations to mankind; it appears to be a valid inference that a good God would also want good for *all* of His creatures.[83] Garcia comes to the conclusion that God employs a very 'low-cost strategy' for engendering belief in His

---

[80] Term employed by Augustine in the *De Libero Arbitrio*.
[81] See Garcia, *St. John of the Cross and the Necessity of Divine Hiddenness*, 2002, p. 85.
[82] Wainwright, *Jonathan Edwards and the Hiddenness of God*, 2002, p. 112.
[83] See Thomas, *Summa*.

existence, and knowledge of how to atone for sin. There definitely appears to be inefficiency in such an enterprise. Is the previous account sufficient in its reasons for God's lack of intervention in the process of conversion to Christianity? We have seen that he offers us help in coming to believe in Him – why does he not do likewise with regard to His Son?

Christians insist that Christ has left a legacy for all of mankind – yet it seems dismissive to then go on to insist that until a certain group of men have accomplished God's goal (in spreading the good news) many who are unenlightened will be lost. Remember that there is no guarantee that the chosen people of God will be successful in their endeavour, as they too are mere men with human weaknesses. However, one may claim that while this may be true with regard to certain aspects of their lives, it is God through grace who will fulfill the dissemination of the gospels, for it is only through God that man does anything meritorious.

Why then does God not speed-up the process? Luther offers the following illumination. When we consider such matters we encounter the

> ...concealed and dreadful will of God, who, by His own design, ordains whom he wills to receive and partake of the mercy preached and offered, and what sort of persons they shall be. This is not to be enquired into, but reverently adored as far as the most awesome secret of the divine majesty, reserved to Himself alone and forbidden to us...[84]

But he encourages us not to despair, for we can be certain that:

> That this is the highest degree of faith to believe that he is merciful who saves so few and damns so many.[85]

However, one can retort that this is a lot more comforting and easy to accept when you are one who has heard of God and Christ, and have been

---

[84] W.A. 18.684.32, in Gerrish, *"To the Unknown God": Luther and Calvin on the Hiddenness of God*, 1973, p. 274.
[85] W.A. 18.633.15. in Gerrish, *"To the Unknown God": Luther and Calvin on the Hiddenness of God* 1973, p. 274.

convinced of the truth of Scripture.

Regarding Christianity, and the damnation of many due to the non-exposure to Christian scriptures, we can only reach one of two conclusions. (i) God wishes a chosen people to be responsible for the conversion of the faithless, for reasons that we are not privy to and which do not conflict with His status as the ultimate personification of love and goodness. There is no logical reason why this should not be the case – we can only attempt to approximate the intentions of God, as the finite mind is incapable of fathoming the infinite mind. Such a belief requires faith that God is merciful, and yet does not personally intervene to save an indefinitely large number of men. We have already seen that many Christians believe that such faith is essential to a meaningful relationship with God. Alternatively, (ii) we can come to the conclusion that it is a result of man's own guilt that he is not saved, and therefore God's acts are just, and as already suggested we should be grateful that He chooses to save anyone at all.

If we are not Christians we may insist that the faith that is necessary for a meaningful relationship with God can be accomplished without exposure to the Christian Scriptures and belief in Christ, that all we need is passionate interest, and not Christianity. Surely, it would appear extremely unjust to any non-Christian theist who has never been exposed to the New Testament, that despite his love of God he can never achieve salvation and union with the divine.

I will now set aside the issue of belief in Christ and engage with the possibility that it is man's own fault if he does not believe in God.

10

Defectiveness

We have already encountered the idea that the reason that many people do not come to believe in the divine is because of some sort of defect that is essential to their nature, rather than being the fault of God, or of the sort of evidence through which He chooses to reveal Himself. Approaches to the hiddenness of God that employ this idea are called 'human-defectiveness theories."

Some Christians claim that God has done more than enough to reveal Himself to us, but it is through a voluntary act of suppression that we remain unenlightened. For this act to be culpable on our part does not require that we be explicitly aware of our activity. In his letter to the Romans, Paul makes such a suggestion – man refuses to acknowledge the truth because of immersion in the material pleasures and concerns of secular existence. As we become increasingly absorbed in the material sensual world, we further blind ourselves to the supra-sensual transcendental realm of spirit. As a result, the internal evidence that God provides is shunned in favour of naturalistic and scientific modes of interpretation, or alternatively man loses any interest in the nature of being and the *meaning* that lies *behind* the world in which he finds himself.

Once again, this theory sheds light on the question of why God does not reveal Himself to all men equally. It may be that God offers *sufficient* evidence for belief to all men, but certain nations and cultures may *en mass* have evolved to a stage of material immersion which excludes the possibility of their recognising and accepting the evidence that God makes freely available to them.

This involves an understanding that all of mankind are communally guilty as a race – while insisting that each man perpetuates that guilt through the actions that he performs in his own life. Thus, it is not a case of the sons being held accountable for the sins of their fathers, for the sons continue to commit those same sins through their own voluntary actions (even if those actions are not explicitly recognised as being sinful. This point has already been justified by establishing that man has a responsibility to seek God, irrespective of his epistemic standing).

The very fact that many believe that we are in a position to adequately deal with the question of God's existence on our own naturalistic terms, can be seen as evidence of the presumptuousness that resides in man's arrogant nature. Such attempts to deal with, and dismiss, the question of hiddenness presume that we are already at a stage of spiritual, moral and intellectual evolution which is appropriate and sufficient for such an investigation. It appears rather conceited for man to imagine that he is reliably equipped to deal with the divine, given his own fallibility and susceptibility to error.[86] In the Book of Genesis, pride was the principal flaw that caused the downfall of Adam.

When we attempt to analyse the divine using the restrictive methodologies of naturalism we are once again duplicating the primordial fall (even if we read this allegorically or symbolically the point is still valid). Adam, as our allegorical father, wished to establish an order that set itself up in opposition to the authority of God, and to the providence that He had decreed for the created world. When we refuse to see any evidence of the divine, we once again wish to establish an order that excludes the need for God and makes us the lords of all that we see. McKim asks:

> How can we avoid the obvious sense that there is a moral deficiency in those who, by their lack of belief in God, demonstrate that they do not even 'desire to see,' and are not willing to live in the presence of God?[87]

This account can be upheld as long as we admit that the fault of our defectiveness originates in our own free action, and that it is not the product of some essential feature of our natures that is beyond our control. For, if we cannot in fact do anything to remedy our blindness, then surely the degree of our culpability must be mitigated or obliterated. If our defectiveness is the cause of divine hiddenness, and if that defectiveness is the product of a freely instigated state of affairs, then we must take responsibility for our failure and accept its ramifications without protest. If this is the case, it is not that God is an obscure God, it is rather that we render the facts about Him obscure.[88]

When we consider the doctrine of the Fall and the Scriptural commentaries on it, we are left with the uneasy feeling that man has inherited the guilt of his forebear and that this has left him cognitively and

---

[86] See Moser, *Cognitive Idolatry and Divine Hiding* , 2002, p. 137.

[87] McKim, *The Hiddenness of God*, 1990 pp. 102-103.

[88] Ibid. p. 145.

conatively injured. After all, if Adam damaged our very natures such that they are now incapable of approaching the divine, then it appears as though there is nothing that man can do about his lamentable position – indeed it seems that he has no responsibility for even failing to recognise his position. However, upon closer inspection we find no evidence in Biblical texts that it is beyond man's capabilities to recognise his deficiencies, if he so endeavours. We can also see no metaphysical or psychological constraints (on non-pathological individuals) from recognising their personal selfishness and moral failures. In fact, although it may require some personal courage to look at one's character neutrally, everyone has at some time in their life realised that morally they are by far inferior to that which they know they could and should be.

The Christian insists that where we find difficulty is in self-rectifying those imperfections. Man is damaged goods, he continues to damage himself – he has it in his power to recognise that he is doing so, and yet he must seek the help of God to alleviate his injuries.

In my earlier discussion, I introduced the idea that man can begin the process of faith – he can attempt to become passionately interested and thereby begin the progression that may eventually lead to divine illumination. The problem that we have with the orthodox conception of grace is that, even though two men may appear to seek God with the same passion, there is no guarantee that both will find God, or that God will offer salvation to both or to either. As we have seen, we can provide no necessary reasons for why God would have any responsibilities to His creatures; all we can offer is an appeal to morality, as we understand it. This is one of the very frustrating situations in which, if we are to maintain faith, we must simply subscribe to the notion that God has reasons for His actions that we cannot fathom. (We might liken it to a person that owns a dog and then meditates on how to treat it – there is no reason other than an appeal to moral standards as to why he should treat it in any specific way. Yet surely we must admit that there are some moral standards to which his behaviour should adhere. If there were something that God should do, then surely He would do it, as he is the ultimate instance of moral perfection. The problem is that we have no standards by which to judge the actions of God other than our own, and given our own imperfections we have seen the arrogance of applying those standards in this instance.)

We might ask why it is that God would permit a man to search in earnest for Him all of his life and yet never permit him belief in the divine. What possible good would this achieve? How would this contribute to the sum of the good? If man is blinded as a punishment for his sin, and the continuation of that sin, it logically follows that God deems loss of sight of the divine as appropriate punishment for man's misdemeanors (see Paul Rom. 1:18-25).[89] But is this the loving God of the Christian that appears to be at work, or is it a wrathful God that seeks vengeance?

It is my contention that punishment should lead to reform, but what is the point of implementing a punishment that will make reform harder and relapse more likely? Furthermore, if man is not even aware that he is being punished, and that this punishment is supposed to act as a deterrent, then what is the point of the exercise? The best explanation once again returns to the points already outlined in this book – man must co-operate in the process of redemption, God has no responsibility for his doing so, God is ultimately just and therefore whatever punishment is meted out is appropriate, and the very proof that God is ultimately merciful is evinced by the fact that he chooses to save *some* as opposed to *none* – for none merit redemption.

As already discussed, the traditional understanding of grace revolves around the idea that it is impossible for man to perform any good work without the aid of God – consequently no man ever deserves salvation. Another possible explanation is that God offers assistance to all those who earnestly seek Him, that grace is equally available to all, it is just that we have no idea what criteria God would employ when qualifying exactly what is entailed in earnestly seeking. After all, this is not a pursuit that can be measured in human standards, for no one knows the internal working of any others mind. Perhaps then, my above example is vacuous, there are never two men who seek God equally, one being rewarded one being denied – each man's pursuit will be significantly unique and will be treated accordingly by God.

This leaves us with one major problem unsolved. Many of my assertions and claims may be true for theists of no particular Church – but I have already referred to the fact that Christians believe that the only method of salvation is through the grace of God and the assistance of Christ. We may be defective and have to accept responsibility for not

---

[89] Keller, *The Hiddenness of God and the Problem of Evil*, 1995, p. 17.

recognising the evidence that God provides for His existence, but individually we cannot be held responsible for not having heard and believed in Christ, if we have never been exposed in any form to the New Testament. Furthermore, in believing in Christ we are asked to believe in an individual to which we cannot independently reason, for while we may have sufficient epistemic warrant for seeing the divine in the created world and the occurrences therein, we can see God in this way without ever seeing Christ. It appears that if God offers evidence of His existence to all men, he does not offer evidence of His Son in the same way.

11
Conclusion

I began this book by attempting to delineate exactly what is involved in the idea that God is hidden. I investigated the specific criteria that would be necessary for a universal disclosure of the existence of God, and asked whether these criteria can ever be successfully satisfied, or whether the very attempt at such a formulation is in itself misguided. I gave a description of miraculous signs and the various ways in which they can be interpreted. The issue of conflicting epistemic standards was considered, and its ramifications for the acceptance of certain states of affairs as evidence discussed. I asked what makes a belief rational and suggested one's epistemic responsibilities when reflecting on information and thereby coming to beliefs. I argued that religious belief is not irrational, and actually has a high epistemic status because it is both prudentially rational and epistemically rational.

I then asked whether it is possible to reach a conversion through an intentional free action of the will, and showed that one can at least begin the process of conversion (the conversion in question is to belief in a monotheistic God of love). I suggested that everyone should attempt to reach an awareness of the divine, because the ultimate well-being of the individual may depend on it. For this reason, I proposed that an interestedness in God should become our ultimate concern – for if there is even the possibility that we have souls, and that our eternal welfare is at stake, this provides sufficient warrant for us to devote our greatest efforts to finding the truth. I provided reasons as to why the naturalist should temporarily suspend the religious doubt engendered by his epistemic standards in the hope of reaching divine illumination. I endeavoured to prove that it is not possible to force oneself to come to belief through a volitional cognitive operation but that through a free action of the will that one can choose to begin a process of faith that may eventually result in belief.

I then proceeded to ask why God does not reveal Himself unambiguously to the masses as a whole. I considered the view that God does not show Himself in this fashion in order to preserve the freedom and individuality of man. I investigated the nature of the coercion that a certain revelation of God might exert. I brought attention to the ways in which the God of Christianity wants us to approach Him, and by implication, the ways in which any supreme God of love would want to form a relationship with His sentient creatures.

I investigated the condition that is love and considered whether it is a volitional state or is causally necessitated. I showed what the appropriate response to love is, why we must be free to reciprocate the love offered to us and where the freedom and the direction of the will resides in this process. I argued that it is in the response that we offer to the one who loves us that there is significant moral freedom. I demonstrated that although God wants everyone to believe in Him, that He wants even more for mankind to love Him, and that therefore the motivation that we have in approaching Him is of the greatest importance. The love that we have for God must be of a certain caliber, as deficiency leads to blindness. I illuminated why this is the reason that man cannot know God with certainty until he has achieved a particular standard.

At this point I returned to the question of the implications that cognitive certainty would have on the freedom of man. I proposed that although cognitive certainty would leave no option as to whether or not man believes in the existence of God, that one would only be forced into notional assent and not real assent. For this reason, I suggested that a certain cognitive disclosure would still leave room for significant freedom in one's response to that knowledge. Following this line of argument, I showed that the school of thought that suggests that a certain disclosure of God's existence would completely obliterate man's freedom to love God is mistaken. I suggested instead that God does not offer certain disclosure because of man's propensity to approach Him for the wrong reasons. Thus, I established that it is the ability to form a free and correct (morally) loving relationship to God that grounds God's epistemic distance and not His attempt to preserve man's freedom.

I proceeded to consider the Christian understanding of grace. I investigated the Christian belief that man can only approach God through Christ, and asked why it is that (the Christian) God has revealed His Scriptures to a greater degree in some cultures. I asked what role man must play in the redemption of the race as a whole and evaluated the different solutions to this problem that have been traditionally offered.

I then reflected on the theory that it is man's own defectiveness that prevents him from recognising the full disclosure of God's existence that is readily made available to him. I showed that by adopting this line of reasoning one can claim that man is free to save himself, or at least to recognise the love of God and embrace it, and can stop suppressing or ignoring the evidence that God constantly makes available. I also highlighted the fact that whilst all men may be to *some extent* morally accountable for not believing in God, not all men can be held morally accountable for not believing in Christ.

Thus, my final conclusion can be summarised as follows: God hides so that man may form an appropriate free and loving response to the love that He offers.

Bibliography:

Aiken, H. D. (1958). God and Evil: a study of some relations between faith and morals. *Ethics*, 68, pp. 77-97.

Digby, T. (1982). On Observability and Detectability. *Religious Studies*, 18, pp. 509-511.

Dilley, F. B. (1977). Fool-Proof Proofs of God? *International Journal for Philosophy of Religion*, 8, pp. 18-35.

Drange, T. (1998). *Nonbelief and Evil*. New York: Prometheus.

Ferreira, M. J. (2002). A Kierkegaardian View of Divine Hiddenness. In Howard-Snyder, D (ed.) & Moser, P. (eds.) (2002).

Garcia, L. L. (2002). St. John of the Cross and the Necessity of Divine Hiddenness. In Howard-Snyder, D (ed.) & Moser, P. (eds.) (2002).

Gerrish, B. A. (1973) "To the Unknown God": Luther and Calvin on the Hiddeness of God. *The Journal of Religion*, 53, pp. 263-292.

Hare, R. M. (1955). *New Essays in Philosophical Theology*. London: S. C. M. Press.

Hick, J. (1964). *The Existence of God*. London: Collier Macmillan Publishers.

Hick, J. (1973). *Philosophy of Religion*. New Jersey: Prentice-Hall Inc.

Hick, J. (1981). *Faith and Knowledge*. Oxford: Clarendon Press.

Howard-Snyder, D. (1996). The Argument from Divine Hiddenness. *Canadian Journal of Philosophy*, 26, pp. 433-453.

Howard-Snyder, D. (2002). Introduction to The Hiddenness of God. In Howard-Snyder, D (ed.) & Moser, P. (eds.) (2002).

Howard-Snyder, D. (ed.) & Moser, P. (eds.) (2002). *Divine Hiddenness*, Cambridge: Cambridge University Press.

Keller, J. A. (1995). The Hiddenness of God and the Problem of Evil. *Philosophy of Religion*, 37, pp. 13-24.

McKim, R. (1990). The Hiddenness of God. *Religious Studies*, 26, pp. 141-161.

Mesle, R. C. (1988). Does God Hide from Us? *International Journal for Philosophy of Religion*, 24, pp. 93-111.

Moser, P. K. (2002). Cognitive Idolatry and Divine Hiding. In Howard-Snyder, D (ed.) & Moser, P. (eds.) (2002).

Murray, M. J. (2002). Deus Absconditus. In Howard-Snyder, D (ed.) & Moser, P. (eds.) (2002).

Newman, John Henry [1870] (1985). An Essay in Aid of a Grammar of Assent. Cambridge: Cambridge University Press.

Ross, J. J. (2002). The Hiddenness of God - A Puzzle or a Real Problem? In Howard-Snyder, D (ed.) & Moser, P. (eds.) (2002).

Rowe, W. (1979). The Problem of Evil and Some Varieties of Atheism. *American Philosophical Quarterly*, 16, 335-341.

Rowe, W. (1982). Religious Experience and the Principle of Credulity. *International Journal for Philosophy of Religion*, 13, pp. 85-92.

Schellenberg, J. L. (1993). *Divine Hiddenness and Human Reason*. Ithaca: Cornell University Press.

Schellenberg, J. L. (2002). *What the Hiddenness of God Reveals*. Cambridge: Cambridge University Press.

Stump, E. & Flint, T. P. (1993). *Hermes and Athena: Biblical Exegesis and Philosophical Theology*. Notre Dame : University of Notre Dame Press.

Tennant, F. R. (1930). *Philosophical Theology*. Cambridge: Cambridge University Press.

Tillich, P. (1951). *Systematic Theology, I*. Chicago: University of Chicago Press.

Tipton, I. (1988). *The Handbook of Western Philosophy*. New York: Macmillan.

Van Inwagen, P. (2002). What is the Problem of the Hiddenness of God? In Howard-Snyder, D (ed.) & Moser, P. (eds.) (2002).

Van Steenberg, F. (1966). *Hidden God, How Do We Know that God Exists?* (trans. Crowley, T.). Missouri: B. Herder Book Co.

Wainwright, W. J. (2002). Jonathan Edwards and the Hiddenness of God. In Howard-Snyder, D (ed.) & Moser, P. (eds.) (2002).

Wisdom, J. (1964). *Philosophy and Psychoanalysis*. Oxford: Basil Blackwell.